everyday calm

everyday calm

peaceful prompts for
tranquil moments

ROCK
POINT

We cannot see our
reflection in running water.
It's only in still water
that we can see.

TAOIST PROVERB

Introduction

Life is a whirlwind, to say the least. With ever-growing lists of responsibilities and to-dos, there never seems to be enough time in the day to accomplish it all, let alone spend time on your own self-care and rejuvenation. But constantly going at full speed with no reprieve can have drastically negative effects on your physical health, your mental state, and your relationships.

With *Everyday Calm*, you can begin to work on repairing the most important relationship of all—the one with yourself. One of the best ways to re-energize and find inner peace is to expel any stress, anxiety, or harmful thoughts through writing, a literal way of drawing out the bad and storing it in someplace other than your body or mind. This journal explores the concept of calm—what it means to live slow, be still, and intimately connect with what's happening to you both internally and externally on a constant basis.

Everyday Calm gives you the opportunity to pinpoint your quiet moments in a few different ways. Get to know yourself and how you do (or don't) decompress through the various prompts in the free writing section. These thoughtful questions help you dig deep to uncover how you are forming your emotional, physical, and mental habits, as well as a big picture view of how you go about keeping calm in your life. To get a more detailed idea of how much peace you are experiencing, you can chart your acts of self-care monthly and carve out time to meditate daily.

Finding your individual sense of calm can have a great impact on how you approach everyday life, improve your treatment of others, and develop your self-care and personal growth.

What can lift your mood?

_____

_____

_____

_____

_____

_____

_____

_____

_____

_____

_____

_____

_____

_____

What are you grateful for?

What is your ideal daily routine?

_____

_____

_____

_____

_____

_____

_____

_____

_____

_____

_____

_____

_____

_____

_____

_____

_____

_____

How would you describe your current level of self-belief?

_____

_____

_____

_____

_____

_____

_____

_____

_____

_____

_____

_____

_____

_____

_____

_____

_____

What boosts your energy?

When do you feel the most confident?

_____

_____

_____

_____

_____

_____

_____

_____

_____

_____

_____

_____

_____

_____

What drains your energy?

_____

_____

_____

_____

_____

_____

_____

_____

_____

_____

_____

_____

_____

What have you achieved recently (no matter how small)?

_____

_____

_____

_____

_____

_____

_____

_____

_____

_____

_____

_____

_____

_____

_____

_____

_____

Physical Habits

Which foods nourish you the most?
When do you feel most physically healthy?

_____

_____

_____

_____

_____

_____

_____

_____

_____

_____

_____

_____

_____

_____

_____

How do you look after your body?

_____

_____

_____

_____

_____

_____

_____

_____

_____

_____

_____

_____

_____

_____

_____

_____

_____

Where and/or when do you feel most at peace?

_____

_____

_____

_____

_____

_____

_____

_____

_____

_____

_____

_____

_____

_____

_____

What do you feel most passionate about?

Mental Habits

When are you in your best headspace?

_____

_____

_____

_____

_____

_____

_____

_____

_____

_____

_____

_____

_____

_____

What are you doing when you're in your perfect state of mind?

_____

_____

_____

_____

_____

_____

_____

_____

_____

_____

_____

_____

_____

_____

_____

_____

At what time of day do you feel mentally energized?

_____

_____

_____

_____

_____

_____

_____

_____

_____

_____

_____

_____

_____

_____

Do you treat yourself as kindly as you treat others?

_____

_____

_____

_____

_____

_____

_____

_____

_____

_____

_____

_____

_____

_____

_____

Work–Life Balance

Fill the jars with words that describe
where your energy is spent.

Monthly Self-Care Plan

Creating good habits requires holding yourself accountable for how much you do or do not stick with your newly created routines and lifestyles.

Just as frequent journaling assists with re-centering yourself and helping you stay grounded, keeping a tracker can help you see whether you achieve your goals consistently, or if you need to reevaluate your processes. Trackers are also great tools to aid in developing self-discipline, and can boost self-esteem when you look back on your logs to see how much you achieved.

As a means for encouraging tranquility in your life, this monthly tracker will help gauge how much time and attention you are giving yourself over the course of one year.

For each month, list your ideal self-care activities. Try to have a good balance of activities that cover your physical, mental, and spiritual well-being. Check off or color in the boxes for each day that you indulge in your favorite things.

At the end of each month, reflect on your list. How many activities did you do and how often did you do them? How did the ways you spent time with yourself differ, and how did you feel afterwards? What, if anything, would you do differently next month?

Month: _____

ACTIVITY

1						
2						
3						
4						
5						
6						
7						
8						
9						
10						
11						
12						
13						
14						
15						
16						
17						
18						
19						
20						
21						
22						
23						
24						
25						
26						
27						
28						
29						
30						
31						

Month:

ACTIVITY						
1						
2						
3						
4						
5						
6						
7						
8						
9						
10						
11						
12						
13						
14						
15						
16						
17						
18						
19						
20						
21						
22						
23						
24						
25						
26						
27						
28						
29						
30						
31						

Month:

ACTIVITY						
1						
2						
3						
4						
5						
6						
7						
8						
9						
10						
11						
12						
13						
14						
15						
16						
17						
18						
19						
20						
21						
22						
23						
24						
25						
26						
27						
28						
29						
30						
31						

Month:

ACTIVITY						
1						
2						
3						
4						
5						
6						
7						
8						
9						
10						
11						
12						
13						
14						
15						
16						
17						
18						
19						
20						
21						
22						
23						
24						
25						
26						
27						
28						
29						
30						
31						

Month:

Activity					
1					
2					
3					
4					
5					
6					
7					
8					
9					
10					
11					
12					
13					
14					
15					
16					
17					
18					
19					
20					
21					
22					
23					
24					
25					
26					
27					
28					
29					
30					
31					

Month:

ACTIVITY

1					
2					
3					
4					
5					
6					
7					
8					
9					
10					
11					
12					
13					
14					
15					
16					
17					
18					
19					
20					
21					
22					
23					
24					
25					
26					
27					
28					
29					
30					
31					

Month:

ACTIVITY

1
2
3
4
5
6
7
8
9
10
11
12
13
14
15
16
17
18
19
20
21
22
23
24
25
26
27
28
29
30
31

Month:

ACTIVITY						
1						
2						
3						
4						
5						
6						
7						
8						
9						
10						
11						
12						
13						
14						
15						
16						
17						
18						
19						
20						
21						
22						
23						
24						
25						
26						
27						
28						
29						
30						
31						

Month:

ACTIVITY						
1						
2						
3						
4						
5						
6						
7						
8						
9						
10						
11						
12						
13						
14						
15						
16						
17						
18						
19						
20						
21						
22						
23						
24						
25						
26						
27						
28						
29						
30						
31						

Month:

ACTIVITY

1					
2					
3					
4					
5					
6					
7					
8					
9					
10					
11					
12					
13					
14					
15					
16					
17					
18					
19					
20					
21					
22					
23					
24					
25					
26					
27					
28					
29					
30					
31					

Month:

ACTIVITY

1						
2						
3						
4						
5						
6						
7						
8						
9						
10						
11						
12						
13						
14						
15						
16						
17						
18						
19						
20						
21						
22						
23						
24						
25						
26						
27						
28						
29						
30						
31						

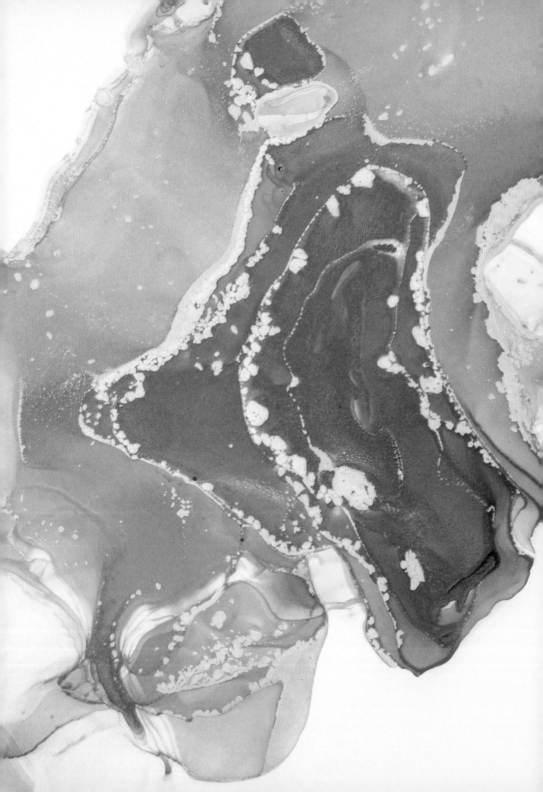

Everyday Calm

DAILY MEDITATIONS

When you think of the practice of meditation, what comes to mind? People on pillows contorted like pretzels? Singing bowls and burning incense? Chants of 'om'? Practicing meditation in this way might seem incredibly intense and unachievable, but the world of meditation isn't meant to be intimidating but rather inspiring and inviting.

The practice of meditation is extremely personal. While there are many examples to guide you, you are always encouraged to forge your own path and practice reflection in a way that speaks to your individual needs and personality.

Once you've decided how to meditate, you'll need to figure out when. This quiet time with yourself should not be seen as a burden, so try not to think of your daily meditation as just one more thing you need to fit into an already overpacked schedule. Instead of making a standing meeting with yourself or blocking off time in a planner, insert your meditation time in a gentle and natural way. Set a soft alarm or ask a friend or family member to remind you to pause during your day. You can even take a looser approach and trust your feelings to only meditate when your body or mind dictates.

The daily meditations here are designed to intentionally slow you down so that you quietly and calmly take stock of your surroundings and the emotions you experience during that time.

Date:

Time:

What's the weather like right now?

_____
_____
_____

List three things you can feel:

1 _____

2 _____

3 _____

List five things you can see:

1 _____

2 _____

3 _____

4 _____

5 _____

List two things you can smell:

1 _____

2 _____

List one thing you can taste:

1 _____

List four things you can hear:

1 _____

2 _____

3 _____

4 _____

Breathe in through your nose
for four seconds, and then out
through your mouth
for another four seconds.
Repeat this four times.

Date:

Time:

What's the weather like right now?

_____

_____

_____

List five things you can see:

1
_____

2
_____

3
_____

4
_____

5
_____

List four things you can hear:

1
_____

2
_____

3
_____

4
_____

List three things you can feel:

1
_____

2
_____

3
_____

List two things you can smell:

1
_____

2
_____

List one thing you can taste:

1
_____

Breathe in through your nose
for four seconds, and then out
through your mouth
for another four seconds.
Repeat this four times.

Date:

Time:

What's the weather like right now?

_____

_____

_____

List three things you can feel:

1

_____

2

_____

3

_____

List five things you can see:

1

_____

2

_____

3

_____

4

_____

5

_____

List two things you can smell:

1

_____

2

_____

List one thing you can taste:

1

_____

List four things you can hear:

1

_____

2

_____

3

_____

4

_____

Breathe in through your nose
for four seconds, and then out
through your mouth
for another four seconds.
Repeat this four times.

Date:

Time:

What's the weather like right now?

_____

_____

_____

List three things you can feel:

1 _____

2 _____

3 _____

List five things you can see:

1 _____

2 _____

3 _____

4 _____

5 _____

List two things you can smell:

1 _____

2 _____

List one thing you can taste:

1 _____

List four things you can hear:

1 _____

2 _____

3 _____

4 _____

Breathe in through your nose
for four seconds, and then out
through your mouth
for another four seconds.
Repeat this four times.

Date:

Time:

What's the weather like right now?

_____

_____

_____

List three things you can feel:

1

_____

2

_____

3

_____

List five things you can see:

1

_____

2

_____

3

_____

4

_____

5

_____

List two things you can smell:

1

_____

2

_____

List one thing you can taste:

1

_____

List four things you can hear:

1

_____

2

_____

3

_____

4

_____

Breathe in through your nose
for four seconds, and then out
through your mouth
for another four seconds.
Repeat this four times.

Date:

Time:

What's the weather like right now?

_____

_____

_____

List three things you can feel:

1 _____

2 _____

3 _____

List five things you can see:

1 _____

2 _____

3 _____

4 _____

5 _____

List two things you can smell:

1 _____

2 _____

List one thing you can taste:

1 _____

List four things you can hear:

1 _____

2 _____

3 _____

4 _____

Breathe in through your nose
for four seconds, and then out
through your mouth
for another four seconds.
Repeat this four times.

Date:

Time:

What's the weather like right now?

_____

_____

_____

List three things you can feel:

1 _____

2 _____

3 _____

List five things you can see:

1 _____

2 _____

3 _____

4 _____

5 _____

List two things you can smell:

1 _____

2 _____

List one thing you can taste:

1 _____

List four things you can hear:

1 _____

2 _____

3 _____

4 _____

Breathe in through your nose
for four seconds, and then out
through your mouth
for another four seconds.
Repeat this four times.

Date:

Time:

What's the weather like right now?

_____

_____

_____

List three things you can feel:

1 _____

2 _____

3 _____

List five things you can see:

1 _____

2 _____

3 _____

4 _____

5 _____

List two things you can smell:

1 _____

2 _____

List one thing you can taste:

1 _____

List four things you can hear:

1 _____

2 _____

3 _____

4 _____

Breathe in through your nose
for four seconds, and then out
through your mouth
for another four seconds.
Repeat this four times.

Date:

Time:

What's the weather like right now?

_____

_____

_____

List three things you can feel:

1 _____

2 _____

3 _____

List five things you can see:

1 _____

2 _____

3 _____

4 _____

5 _____

List two things you can smell:

1 _____

2 _____

List one thing you can taste:

1 _____

List four things you can hear:

1 _____

2 _____

3 _____

4 _____

Breathe in through your nose
for four seconds, and then out
through your mouth
for another four seconds.
Repeat this four times.

Date:

Time:

What's the weather like right now?

_____
_____
_____

List three things you can feel:

1 _____

2 _____

3 _____

List five things you can see:

1 _____

2 _____

3 _____

4 _____

5 _____

List two things you can smell:

1 _____

2 _____

List one thing you can taste:

1 _____

List four things you can hear:

1 _____

2 _____

3 _____

4 _____

Breathe in through your nose
for four seconds, and then out
through your mouth
for another four seconds.
Repeat this four times.

Date:

Time:

What's the weather like right now?

_____
_____
_____
_____

List three things you can feel:

1 _____

2 _____

3 _____

List five things you can see:

1 _____

2 _____

3 _____

4 _____

5 _____

List two things you can smell:

1 _____

2 _____

List one thing you can taste:

1 _____

List four things you can hear:

1 _____

2 _____

3 _____

4 _____

Breathe in through your nose
for four seconds, and then out
through your mouth
for another four seconds.
Repeat this four times.

Date:

Time:

What's the weather like right now?

_____

_____

_____

List three things you can feel:

1
_____

2
_____

3
_____

List five things you can see:

1
_____

2
_____

3
_____

4
_____

5
_____

List two things you can smell:

1
_____

2
_____

List one thing you can taste:

1
_____

List four things you can hear:

1
_____

2
_____

3
_____

4
_____

Breathe in through your nose
for four seconds, and then out
through your mouth
for another four seconds.
Repeat this four times.

Date:

Time:

What's the weather like right now?

_____

_____

_____

List three things you can feel:

1
_____

2
_____

3
_____

List five things you can see:

1
_____

2
_____

3
_____

4
_____

5
_____

List two things you can smell:

1
_____

2
_____

List one thing you can taste:

1
_____

List four things you can hear:

1
_____

2
_____

3
_____

4
_____

Breathe in through your nose
for four seconds, and then out
through your mouth
for another four seconds.
Repeat this four times.

Date:

Time:

What's the weather like right now?

_____

_____

_____

List three things you can feel:

1
_____

2
_____

3
_____

List five things you can see:

1
_____

2
_____

3
_____

4
_____

5
_____

List two things you can smell:

1
_____

2
_____

List one thing you can taste:

1
_____

List four things you can hear:

1
_____

2
_____

3
_____

4
_____

Breathe in through your nose
for four seconds, and then out
through your mouth
for another four seconds.
Repeat this four times.

Date:

Time:

What's the weather like right now?

_____

_____

_____

List three things you can feel:

1

_____

2

_____

3

_____

List five things you can see:

1

_____

2

_____

3

_____

4

_____

5

_____

List two things you can smell:

1

_____

2

_____

List one thing you can taste:

1

_____

List four things you can hear:

1

_____

2

_____

3

_____

4

_____

Breathe in through your nose
for four seconds, and then out
through your mouth
for another four seconds.
Repeat this four times.

Date:

Time:

What's the weather like right now?

_____

_____

_____

List three things you can feel:

1 _____

2 _____

3 _____

List five things you can see:

1 _____

2 _____

3 _____

4 _____

5 _____

List two things you can smell:

1 _____

2 _____

List one thing you can taste:

1 _____

List four things you can hear:

1 _____

2 _____

3 _____

4 _____

Breathe in through your nose
for four seconds, and then out
through your mouth
for another four seconds.
Repeat this four times.

Date:

Time:

What's the weather like right now?

_____

_____

_____

List three things you can feel:

1
_____

2
_____

3
_____

List five things you can see:

1
_____

2
_____

3
_____

4
_____

5
_____

List two things you can smell:

1
_____

2
_____

List one thing you can taste:

1
_____

List four things you can hear:

1
_____

2
_____

3
_____

4
_____

Breathe in through your nose
for four seconds, and then out
through your mouth
for another four seconds.
Repeat this four times.

Date:

Time:

What's the weather like right now?

_____

_____

_____

List five things you can see:

1 _____

2 _____

3 _____

4 _____

5 _____

List four things you can hear:

1 _____

2 _____

3 _____

4 _____

List three things you can feel:

1 _____

2 _____

3 _____

List two things you can smell:

1 _____

2 _____

List one thing you can taste:

1 _____

Breathe in through your nose
for four seconds, and then out
through your mouth
for another four seconds.
Repeat this four times.

Date:

Time:

What's the weather like right now?

_____
_____
_____

List three things you can feel:

1
_____
2
_____
3
_____

List five things you can see:

1
_____
2
_____
3
_____
4
_____
5
_____

List two things you can smell:

1
_____
2
_____

List one thing you can taste:

1
_____

List four things you can hear:

1
_____
2
_____
3
_____
4
_____

Breathe in through your nose
for four seconds, and then out
through your mouth
for another four seconds.
Repeat this four times.

ate:

me:

What's the weather like right now?

_____

_____

_____

List three things you can feel:

1
_____

2
_____

3
_____

List five things you can see:

1
_____

2
_____

3
_____

4
_____

5
_____

List two things you can smell:

1
_____

2
_____

List one thing you can taste:

1
_____

List four things you can hear:

1
_____

2
_____

3
_____

4
_____

Breathe in through your nose
for four seconds, and then out
through your mouth
for another four seconds.
Repeat this four times.

Date:

Time:

What's the weather like right now?

_____

_____

_____

List three things you can feel:

1 _____

2 _____

3 _____

List five things you can see:

1 _____

2 _____

3 _____

4 _____

5 _____

List two things you can smell:

1 _____

2 _____

List one thing you can taste:

1 _____

List four things you can hear:

1 _____

2 _____

3 _____

4 _____

Breathe in through your nose
for four seconds, and then out
through your mouth
for another four seconds.
Repeat this four times.

Date:

Time:

What's the weather like right now?

_____

_____

_____

List three things you can feel:

1 _____

2 _____

3 _____

List five things you can see:

1 _____

2 _____

3 _____

4 _____

5 _____

List two things you can smell:

1 _____

2 _____

List one thing you can taste:

1 _____

List four things you can hear:

1 _____

2 _____

3 _____

4 _____

Breathe in through your nose
for four seconds, and then out
through your mouth
for another four seconds.
Repeat this four times.

Date:

Time:

What's the weather like right now?

_____

_____

_____

_____

List three things you can feel:

1 _____

2 _____

3 _____

List five things you can see:

1 _____

2 _____

3 _____

4 _____

5 _____

List two things you can smell:

1 _____

2 _____

List one thing you can taste:

1 _____

List four things you can hear:

1 _____

2 _____

3 _____

4 _____

Breathe in through your nose
for four seconds, and then out
through your mouth
for another four seconds.
Repeat this four times.

Date:

Time:

What's the weather like right now?

_____

_____

_____

List five things you can see:

1
_____

2
_____

3
_____

4
_____

5
_____

List four things you can hear:

1
_____

2
_____

3
_____

4
_____

List three things you can feel:

1
_____

2
_____

3
_____

List two things you can smell:

1
_____

2
_____

List one thing you can taste:

1
_____

Breathe in through your nose
for four seconds, and then out
through your mouth
for another four seconds.
Repeat this four times.

Date:

Time:

What's the weather like right now?

_____
_____
_____

List three things you can feel:

1 _____

2 _____

3 _____

List five things you can see:

1 _____

2 _____

3 _____

4 _____

5 _____

List two things you can smell:

1 _____

2 _____

List one thing you can taste:

1 _____

List four things you can hear:

1 _____

2 _____

3 _____

4 _____

Breathe in through your nose
for four seconds, and then out
through your mouth
for another four seconds.
Repeat this four times.

Date:

Time:

What's the weather like right now?

_____

_____

_____

List five things you can see:

1 _____

2 _____

3 _____

4 _____

5 _____

List four things you can hear:

1 _____

2 _____

3 _____

4 _____

List three things you can feel:

1 _____

2 _____

3 _____

List two things you can smell:

1 _____

2 _____

List one thing you can taste:

1 _____

Breathe in through your nose
for four seconds, and then out
through your mouth
for another four seconds.
Repeat this four times.

Date:

Time:

What's the weather like right now?

_____

_____

_____

List three things you can feel:

1 _____

2 _____

3 _____

List five things you can see:

1 _____

2 _____

3 _____

4 _____

5 _____

List two things you can smell:

1 _____

2 _____

List one thing you can taste:

1 _____

List four things you can hear:

1 _____

2 _____

3 _____

4 _____

Breathe in through your nose
for four seconds, and then out
through your mouth
for another four seconds.
Repeat this four times.

Date:

Time:

What's the weather like right now?

_____

_____

_____

List three things you can feel:

1 _____

2 _____

3 _____

List five things you can see:

1 _____

2 _____

3 _____

4 _____

5 _____

List two things you can smell:

1 _____

2 _____

List one thing you can taste:

1 _____

List four things you can hear:

1 _____

2 _____

3 _____

4 _____

Breathe in through your nose
for four seconds, and then out
through your mouth
for another four seconds.
Repeat this four times.

Date:

Time:

What's the weather like right now?

_____

_____

_____

List three things you can feel:

1

_____

2

_____

3

_____

List five things you can see:

1

_____

2

_____

3

_____

4

_____

5

_____

List two things you can smell:

1

_____

2

_____

List one thing you can taste:

1

_____

List four things you can hear:

1

_____

2

_____

3

_____

4

_____

Breathe in through your nose
for four seconds, and then out
through your mouth
for another four seconds.
Repeat this four times.

Date:

Time:

What's the weather like right now?

_____

_____

_____

List three things you can feel:

1 _____

2 _____

3 _____

List five things you can see:

1 _____

2 _____

3 _____

4 _____

5 _____

List two things you can smell:

1 _____

2 _____

List one thing you can taste:

1 _____

List four things you can hear:

1 _____

2 _____

3 _____

4 _____

Breathe in through your nose
for four seconds, and then out
through your mouth
for another four seconds.
Repeat this four times.

Date:

Time:

What's the weather like right now?

_____

_____

_____

List three things you can feel:

1
_____

2
_____

3
_____

List five things you can see:

1
_____

2
_____

3
_____

4
_____

5
_____

List two things you can smell:

1
_____

2
_____

List one thing you can taste:

1
_____

List four things you can hear:

1
_____

2
_____

3
_____

4
_____

Breathe in through your nose
for four seconds, and then out
through your mouth
for another four seconds.
Repeat this four times.

Date:

Time:

What's the weather like right now?

_____

_____

_____

List three things you can feel:

1 _____

2 _____

3 _____

List five things you can see:

1 _____

2 _____

3 _____

4 _____

5 _____

List two things you can smell:

1 _____

2 _____

List one thing you can taste:

1 _____

List four things you can hear:

1 _____

2 _____

3 _____

4 _____

Breathe in through your nose
for four seconds, and then out
through your mouth
for another four seconds.
Repeat this four times.

Date:

Time:

What's the weather like right now?

_____

_____

_____

List five things you can see:

1
_____

2
_____

3
_____

4
_____

5
_____

List four things you can hear:

1
_____

2
_____

3
_____

4
_____

List three things you can feel:

1
_____

2
_____

3
_____

List two things you can smell:

1
_____

2
_____

List one thing you can taste:

1
_____

Breathe in through your nose
for four seconds, and then out
through your mouth
for another four seconds.
Repeat this four times.

Date:

Time:

What's the weather like right now?

_____

_____

_____

List three things you can feel:

1 _____

2 _____

3 _____

List five things you can see:

1 _____

2 _____

3 _____

4 _____

5 _____

List two things you can smell:

1 _____

2 _____

List one thing you can taste:

1 _____

List four things you can hear:

1 _____

2 _____

3 _____

4 _____

Breathe in through your nose
for four seconds, and then out
through your mouth
for another four seconds.
Repeat this four times.

Date:

Time:

What's the weather like right now?

_____

_____

_____

List five things you can see:

1
_____

2
_____

3
_____

4
_____

5
_____

List four things you can hear:

1
_____

2
_____

3
_____

4
_____

List three things you can feel:

1
_____

2
_____

3
_____

List two things you can smell:

1
_____

2
_____

List one thing you can taste:

1
_____

Breathe in through your nose
for four seconds, and then out
through your mouth
for another four seconds.
Repeat this four times.

Date:

Time:

What's the weather like right now?

_____

_____

_____

List three things you can feel:

1 _____

2 _____

3 _____

List five things you can see:

1 _____

2 _____

3 _____

4 _____

5 _____

List two things you can smell:

1 _____

2 _____

List one thing you can taste:

1 _____

List four things you can hear:

1 _____

2 _____

3 _____

4 _____

Breathe in through your nose
for four seconds, and then out
through your mouth
for another four seconds.
Repeat this four times.

Date:

Time:

What's the weather like right now?

_____

_____

_____

List three things you can feel:

1 _____

2 _____

3 _____

List five things you can see:

1 _____

2 _____

3 _____

4 _____

5 _____

List two things you can smell:

1 _____

2 _____

List one thing you can taste:

1 _____

List four things you can hear:

1 _____

2 _____

3 _____

4 _____

Breathe in through your nose
for four seconds, and then out
through your mouth
for another four seconds.
Repeat this four times.

Date:

Time:

What's the weather like right now?

_____

_____

_____

List three things you can feel:

1
_____

2
_____

3
_____

List five things you can see:

1
_____

2
_____

3
_____

4
_____

5
_____

List two things you can smell:

1
_____

2
_____

List one thing you can taste:

1
_____

List four things you can hear:

1
_____

2
_____

3
_____

4
_____

Breathe in through your nose
for four seconds, and then out
through your mouth
for another four seconds.
Repeat this four times.

Date:

Time:

What's the weather like right now?

_____

_____

_____

_____

List three things you can feel:

1

_____

2

_____

3

_____

List five things you can see:

1

_____

2

_____

3

_____

4

_____

5

_____

List two things you can smell:

1

_____

2

_____

List one thing you can taste:

1

_____

List four things you can hear:

1

_____

2

_____

3

_____

4

_____

Breathe in through your nose
for four seconds, and then out
through your mouth
for another four seconds.
Repeat this four times.

Date:

Time:

What's the weather like right now?

_____

_____

_____

List three things you can feel:

1 _____

2 _____

3 _____

List five things you can see:

1 _____

2 _____

3 _____

4 _____

5 _____

List two things you can smell:

1 _____

2 _____

List one thing you can taste:

1 _____

List four things you can hear:

1 _____

2 _____

3 _____

4 _____

Breathe in through your nose
for four seconds, and then out
through your mouth
for another four seconds.
Repeat this four times.

Date:

Time:

What's the weather like right now?

_____

_____

_____

List three things you can feel:

1

_____

2

_____

3

_____

List five things you can see:

1

_____

2

_____

3

_____

4

_____

5

_____

List two things you can smell:

1

_____

2

_____

List one thing you can taste:

1

_____

List four things you can hear:

1

_____

2

_____

3

_____

4

_____

Breathe in through your nose
for four seconds, and then out
through your mouth
for another four seconds.
Repeat this four times.

Date:

Time:

What's the weather like right now?

_____

_____

_____

List three things you can feel:

1 _____

2 _____

3 _____

List five things you can see:

1 _____

2 _____

3 _____

4 _____

5 _____

List two things you can smell:

1 _____

2 _____

List one thing you can taste:

1 _____

List four things you can hear:

1 _____

2 _____

3 _____

4 _____

Breathe in through your nose
for four seconds, and then out
through your mouth
for another four seconds.
Repeat this four times.

Date:

Time:

What's the weather like right now?

_____

_____

_____

List three things you can feel:

1 _____

2 _____

3 _____

List five things you can see:

1 _____

2 _____

3 _____

4 _____

5 _____

List two things you can smell:

1 _____

2 _____

List one thing you can taste:

1 _____

List four things you can hear:

1 _____

2 _____

3 _____

4 _____

Breathe in through your nose
for four seconds, and then out
through your mouth
for another four seconds.
Repeat this four times.

Date:

Time:

What's the weather like right now?

_____

_____

_____

List five things you can see:

1 _____

2 _____

3 _____

4 _____

5 _____

List four things you can hear:

1 _____

2 _____

3 _____

4 _____

List three things you can feel:

1 _____

2 _____

3 _____

List two things you can smell:

1 _____

2 _____

List one thing you can taste:

1 _____

Breathe in through your nose
for four seconds, and then out
through your mouth
for another four seconds.
Repeat this four times.

Date:

Time:

What's the weather like right now?

_____

_____

_____

List five things you can see:

1
_____

2
_____

3
_____

4
_____

5
_____

List four things you can hear:

1
_____

2
_____

3
_____

4
_____

List three things you can feel:

1
_____

2
_____

3
_____

List two things you can smell:

1
_____

2
_____

List one thing you can taste:

1
_____

Breathe in through your nose
for four seconds, and then out
through your mouth
for another four seconds.
Repeat this four times.

Date:

Time:

What's the weather like right now?

_____

_____

_____

List three things you can feel:

1 _____

2 _____

3 _____

List five things you can see:

1 _____

2 _____

3 _____

4 _____

5 _____

List two things you can smell:

1 _____

2 _____

List one thing you can taste:

1 _____

List four things you can hear:

1 _____

2 _____

3 _____

4 _____

Breathe in through your nose
for four seconds, and then out
through your mouth
for another four seconds.
Repeat this four times.

Date:

Time:

What's the weather like right now?

_____

_____

_____

List five things you can see:

1
_____

2
_____

3
_____

4
_____

5
_____

List four things you can hear:

1
_____

2
_____

3
_____

4
_____

List three things you can feel:

1
_____

2
_____

3
_____

List two things you can smell:

1
_____

2
_____

List one thing you can taste:

1
_____

Breathe in through your nose
for four seconds, and then out
through your mouth
for another four seconds.
Repeat this four times.

Date:

Time:

What's the weather like right now?

_____

_____

_____

List three things you can feel:

1 _____

2 _____

3 _____

List five things you can see:

1 _____

2 _____

3 _____

4 _____

5 _____

List two things you can smell:

1 _____

2 _____

List one thing you can taste:

1 _____

List four things you can hear:

1 _____

2 _____

3 _____

4 _____

Breathe in through your nose
for four seconds, and then out
through your mouth
for another four seconds.
Repeat this four times.

Date:

Time:

What's the weather like right now?

_____

_____

_____

List three things you can feel:

1 _____

2 _____

3 _____

List five things you can see:

1 _____

2 _____

3 _____

4 _____

5 _____

List two things you can smell:

1 _____

2 _____

List one thing you can taste:

1 _____

List four things you can hear:

1 _____

2 _____

3 _____

4 _____

Breathe in through your nose
for four seconds, and then out
through your mouth
for another four seconds.
Repeat this four times.

ate:

me:

What's the weather like right now?

_____

_____

_____

List five things you can see:

1

_____

2

_____

3

_____

4

_____

5

_____

List four things you can hear:

1

_____

2

_____

3

_____

4

_____

List three things you can feel:

1

_____

2

_____

3

_____

List two things you can smell:

1

_____

2

_____

List one thing you can taste:

1

_____

Breathe in through your nose
for four seconds, and then out
through your mouth
for another four seconds.
Repeat this four times.

Date:

Time:

What's the weather like right now?

_____

_____

_____

List three things you can feel:

1 _____

2 _____

3 _____

List five things you can see:

1 _____

2 _____

3 _____

4 _____

5 _____

List two things you can smell:

1 _____

2 _____

List one thing you can taste:

1 _____

List four things you can hear:

1 _____

2 _____

3 _____

4 _____

Breathe in through your nose
for four seconds, and then out
through your mouth
for another four seconds.
Repeat this four times.

Date:

Time:

What's the weather like right now?

_____

_____

_____

List three things you can feel:

1

_____

2

_____

3

_____

List five things you can see:

1

_____

2

_____

3

_____

4

_____

5

_____

List two things you can smell:

1

_____

2

_____

List one thing you can taste:

1

_____

List four things you can hear:

1

_____

2

_____

3

_____

4

_____

Breathe in through your nose
for four seconds, and then out
through your mouth
for another four seconds.
Repeat this four times.

Date:

Time:

What's the weather like right now?

_____

_____

_____

List three things you can feel:

1 _____

2 _____

3 _____

List five things you can see:

1 _____

2 _____

3 _____

4 _____

5 _____

List two things you can smell:

1 _____

2 _____

List one thing you can taste:

1 _____

List four things you can hear:

1 _____

2 _____

3 _____

4 _____

Breathe in through your nose
for four seconds, and then out
through your mouth
for another four seconds.
Repeat this four times.

Date:

Time:

What's the weather like right now?

_____

_____

_____

List three things you can feel:

1
_____
2
_____
3
_____

List five things you can see:

1
_____
2
_____
3
_____
4
_____
5
_____

List two things you can smell:

1
_____
2
_____

List one thing you can taste:

1
_____

List four things you can hear:

1
_____
2
_____
3
_____
4
_____

Breathe in through your nose
for four seconds, and then out
through your mouth
for another four seconds.
Repeat this four times.

Date:

Time:

What's the weather like right now?

_____

_____

_____

List three things you can feel:

1 _____

2 _____

3 _____

List five things you can see:

1 _____

2 _____

3 _____

4 _____

5 _____

List two things you can smell:

1 _____

2 _____

List one thing you can taste:

1 _____

List four things you can hear:

1 _____

2 _____

3 _____

4 _____

Breathe in through your nose
for four seconds, and then out
through your mouth
for another four seconds.
Repeat this four times.

Date:

Time:

What's the weather like right now?

_____

_____

_____

List five things you can see:

1
_____

2
_____

3
_____

4
_____

5
_____

List four things you can hear:

1
_____

2
_____

3
_____

4
_____

List three things you can feel:

1
_____

2
_____

3
_____

List two things you can smell:

1
_____

2
_____

List one thing you can taste:

1
_____

Breathe in through your nose
for four seconds, and then out
through your mouth
for another four seconds.
Repeat this four times.

Date:

Time:

What's the weather like right now?

_____

_____

_____

List five things you can see:

1
_____

2
_____

3
_____

4
_____

5
_____

List four things you can hear:

1
_____

2
_____

3
_____

4
_____

List three things you can feel:

1
_____

2
_____

3
_____

List two things you can smell:

1
_____

2
_____

List one thing you can taste:

1
_____

Breathe in through your nose
for four seconds, and then out
through your mouth
for another four seconds.
Repeat this four times.

Date:

Time:

What's the weather like right now?

_____

_____

_____

List three things you can feel:

1
_____

2
_____

3
_____

List five things you can see:

1
_____

2
_____

3
_____

4
_____

5
_____

List two things you can smell:

1
_____

2
_____

List one thing you can taste:

1
_____

List four things you can hear:

1
_____

2
_____

3
_____

4
_____

Breathe in through your nose
for four seconds, and then out
through your mouth
for another four seconds.
Repeat this four times.

Date:

Time:

What's the weather like right now?

_____

_____

_____

_____

List five things you can see:

1 _____

2 _____

3 _____

4 _____

5 _____

List four things you can hear:

1 _____

2 _____

3 _____

4 _____

List three things you can feel:

1 _____

2 _____

3 _____

List two things you can smell:

1 _____

2 _____

List one thing you can taste:

1 _____

Breathe in through your nose
for four seconds, and then out
through your mouth
for another four seconds.
Repeat this four times.

Date:

Time:

What's the weather like right now?

_____

_____

_____

List five things you can see:

1 _____

2 _____

3 _____

4 _____

5 _____

List four things you can hear:

1 _____

2 _____

3 _____

4 _____

List three things you can feel:

1 _____

2 _____

3 _____

List two things you can smell:

1 _____

2 _____

List one thing you can taste:

1 _____

Breathe in through your nose
for four seconds, and then out
through your mouth
for another four seconds.
Repeat this four times.

Date:

Time:

What's the weather like right now?

_____

_____

_____

List three things you can feel:

1

_____

2

_____

3

_____

List five things you can see:

1

_____

2

_____

3

_____

4

_____

5

_____

List two things you can smell:

1

_____

2

_____

List one thing you can taste:

1

_____

List four things you can hear:

1

_____

2

_____

3

_____

4

_____

Breathe in through your nose
for four seconds, and then out
through your mouth
for another four seconds.
Repeat this four times.

Date:

Time:

What's the weather like right now?

_____

_____

_____

List three things you can feel:

1

_____

2

_____

3

_____

List five things you can see:

1

_____

2

_____

3

_____

4

_____

5

_____

List two things you can smell:

1

_____

2

_____

List one thing you can taste:

1

_____

List four things you can hear:

1

_____

2

_____

3

_____

4

_____

Breathe in through your nose for four seconds, and then out through your mouth for another four seconds. Repeat this four times.

Date:

Time:

What's the weather like right now?

_____

_____

_____

List three things you can feel:

1 _____

2 _____

3 _____

List five things you can see:

1 _____

2 _____

3 _____

4 _____

5 _____

List two things you can smell:

1 _____

2 _____

List one thing you can taste:

1 _____

List four things you can hear:

1 _____

2 _____

3 _____

4 _____

Breathe in through your nose
for four seconds, and then out
through your mouth
for another four seconds.
Repeat this four times.

Date:

Time:

What's the weather like right now?

_____

_____

_____

List five things you can see:

1
_____

2
_____

3
_____

4
_____

5
_____

List four things you can hear:

1
_____

2
_____

3
_____

4
_____

List three things you can feel:

1
_____

2
_____

3
_____

List two things you can smell:

1
_____

2
_____

List one thing you can taste:

1
_____

Breathe in through your nose
for four seconds, and then out
through your mouth
for another four seconds.
Repeat this four times.

Date:

Time:

What's the weather like right now?

_____

_____

_____

List three things you can feel:

1 _____

2 _____

3 _____

List five things you can see:

1 _____

2 _____

3 _____

4 _____

5 _____

List two things you can smell:

1 _____

2 _____

List one thing you can taste:

1 _____

List four things you can hear:

1 _____

2 _____

3 _____

4 _____

Breathe in through your nose
for four seconds, and then out
through your mouth
for another four seconds.
Repeat this four times.

Date:

Time:

What's the weather like right now?

_____

_____

_____

List three things you can feel:

1 _____

2 _____

3 _____

List five things you can see:

1 _____

2 _____

3 _____

4 _____

5 _____

List two things you can smell:

1 _____

2 _____

List one thing you can taste:

1 _____

List four things you can hear:

1 _____

2 _____

3 _____

4 _____

Breathe in through your nose
for four seconds, and then out
through your mouth
for another four seconds.
Repeat this four times.

Date:

Time:

What's the weather like right now?

_____

_____

_____

List three things you can feel:

1 _____

2 _____

3 _____

List five things you can see:

1 _____

2 _____

3 _____

4 _____

5 _____

List two things you can smell:

1 _____

2 _____

List one thing you can taste:

1 _____

List four things you can hear:

1 _____

2 _____

3 _____

4 _____

Breathe in through your nose
for four seconds, and then out
through your mouth
for another four seconds.
Repeat this four times.

Date:

Time:

What's the weather like right now?

_____

_____

_____

List five things you can see:

1 _____

2 _____

3 _____

4 _____

5 _____

List four things you can hear:

1 _____

2 _____

3 _____

4 _____

List three things you can feel:

1 _____

2 _____

3 _____

List two things you can smell:

1 _____

2 _____

List one thing you can taste:

1 _____

Breathe in through your nose
for four seconds, and then out
through your mouth
for another four seconds.
Repeat this four times.

Date:

Time:

What's the weather like right now?

_____

_____

_____

List three things you can feel:

1
_____

2
_____

3
_____

List five things you can see:

1
_____

2
_____

3
_____

4
_____

5
_____

List two things you can smell:

1
_____

2
_____

List one thing you can taste:

1
_____

List four things you can hear:

1
_____

2
_____

3
_____

4
_____

Breathe in through your nose
for four seconds, and then out
through your mouth
for another four seconds.
Repeat this four times.

Date:

Time:

What's the weather like right now?

_____

_____

_____

List three things you can feel:

1 _____

2 _____

3 _____

List five things you can see:

1 _____

2 _____

3 _____

4 _____

5 _____

List two things you can smell:

1 _____

2 _____

List one thing you can taste:

1 _____

List four things you can hear:

1 _____

2 _____

3 _____

4 _____

Breathe in through your nose
for four seconds, and then out
through your mouth
for another four seconds.
Repeat this four times.

Date:

Time:

What's the weather like right now?

_____

_____

_____

List three things you can feel:

1 _____

2 _____

3 _____

List five things you can see:

1 _____

2 _____

3 _____

4 _____

5 _____

List two things you can smell:

1 _____

2 _____

List one thing you can taste:

1 _____

List four things you can hear:

1 _____

2 _____

3 _____

4 _____

Breathe in through your nose
for four seconds, and then out
through your mouth
for another four seconds.
Repeat this four times.

Date:

Time:

What's the weather like right now?

_____

_____

_____

List three things you can feel:

1 _____

2 _____

3 _____

List five things you can see:

1 _____

2 _____

3 _____

4 _____

5 _____

List two things you can smell:

1 _____

2 _____

List one thing you can taste:

1 _____

List four things you can hear:

1 _____

2 _____

3 _____

4 _____

Breathe in through your nose
for four seconds, and then out
through your mouth
for another four seconds.
Repeat this four times.

Date:

Time:

What's the weather like right now?

_____

_____

_____

List three things you can feel:

1 _____

2 _____

3 _____

List five things you can see:

1 _____

2 _____

3 _____

4 _____

5 _____

List two things you can smell:

1 _____

2 _____

List one thing you can taste:

1 _____

List four things you can hear:

1 _____

2 _____

3 _____

4 _____

Breathe in through your nose
for four seconds, and then out
through your mouth
for another four seconds.
Repeat this four times.

Date:

Time:

What's the weather like right now?

_____

_____

_____

List five things you can see:

1 _____

2 _____

3 _____

4 _____

5 _____

List four things you can hear:

1 _____

2 _____

3 _____

4 _____

List three things you can feel:

1 _____

2 _____

3 _____

List two things you can smell:

1 _____

2 _____

List one thing you can taste:

1 _____

Breathe in through your nose
for four seconds, and then out
through your mouth
for another four seconds.
Repeat this four times.

Date:

Time:

What's the weather like right now?

_____

_____

_____

List three things you can feel:

1 _____

2 _____

3 _____

List five things you can see:

1 _____

2 _____

3 _____

4 _____

5 _____

List two things you can smell:

1 _____

2 _____

List one thing you can taste:

1 _____

List four things you can hear:

1 _____

2 _____

3 _____

4 _____

Breathe in through your nose
for four seconds, and then out
through your mouth
for another four seconds.
Repeat this four times.

Date:

Time:

What's the weather like right now?

_____
_____
_____

List three things you can feel:

1 _____

2 _____

3 _____

List five things you can see:

1 _____

2 _____

3 _____

4 _____

5 _____

List two things you can smell:

1 _____

2 _____

List one thing you can taste:

1 _____

List four things you can hear:

1 _____

2 _____

3 _____

4 _____

Breathe in through your nose
for four seconds, and then out
through your mouth
for another four seconds.
Repeat this four times.

Date:

Time:

What's the weather like right now?

_____

_____

_____

List five things you can see:

1
_____

2
_____

3
_____

4
_____

5
_____

List four things you can hear:

1
_____

2
_____

3
_____

4
_____

List three things you can feel:

1
_____

2
_____

3
_____

List two things you can smell:

1
_____

2
_____

List one thing you can taste:

1
_____

Breathe in through your nose
for four seconds, and then out
through your mouth
for another four seconds.
Repeat this four times.

Date:

Time:

What's the weather like right now?

_____

_____

_____

List five things you can see:

1
_____

2
_____

3
_____

4
_____

5
_____

List four things you can hear:

1
_____

2
_____

3
_____

4
_____

List three things you can feel:

1
_____

2
_____

3
_____

List two things you can smell:

1
_____

2
_____

List one thing you can taste:

1
_____

Breathe in through your nose
for four seconds, and then out
through your mouth
for another four seconds.
Repeat this four times.

Date:

Time:

What's the weather like right now?

_____

_____

_____

List three things you can feel:

1 _____

2 _____

3 _____

List five things you can see:

1 _____

2 _____

3 _____

4 _____

5 _____

List two things you can smell:

1 _____

2 _____

List one thing you can taste:

1 _____

List four things you can hear:

1 _____

2 _____

3 _____

4 _____

Breathe in through your nose
for four seconds, and then out
through your mouth
for another four seconds.
Repeat this four times.

Date:

Time:

What's the weather like right now?

_____

_____

_____

List three things you can feel:

1 _____

2 _____

3 _____

List five things you can see:

1 _____

2 _____

3 _____

4 _____

5 _____

List two things you can smell:

1 _____

2 _____

List one thing you can taste:

1 _____

List four things you can hear:

1 _____

2 _____

3 _____

4 _____

Breathe in through your nose
for four seconds, and then out
through your mouth
for another four seconds.
Repeat this four times.

Date:

Time:

What's the weather like right now?

_____

_____

_____

List three things you can feel:

1

_____

2

_____

3

_____

List five things you can see:

1

_____

2

_____

3

_____

4

_____

5

_____

List two things you can smell:

1

_____

2

_____

List one thing you can taste:

1

_____

List four things you can hear:

1

_____

2

_____

3

_____

4

_____

Breathe in through your nose
for four seconds, and then out
through your mouth
for another four seconds.
Repeat this four times.

Date:

Time:

What's the weather like right now?

_____

_____

_____

List five things you can see:

1
_____

2
_____

3
_____

4
_____

5
_____

List four things you can hear:

1
_____

2
_____

3
_____

4
_____

List three things you can feel:

1
_____

2
_____

3
_____

List two things you can smell:

1
_____

2
_____

List one thing you can taste:

1
_____

Breathe in through your nose
for four seconds, and then out
through your mouth
for another four seconds.
Repeat this four times.

Date:

Time:

What's the weather like right now?

_____
_____
_____

List three things you can feel:

1 _____

2 _____

3 _____

List five things you can see:

1 _____

2 _____

3 _____

4 _____

5 _____

List two things you can smell:

1 _____

2 _____

List one thing you can taste:

1 _____

List four things you can hear:

1 _____

2 _____

3 _____

4 _____

Breathe in through your nose
for four seconds, and then out
through your mouth
for another four seconds.
Repeat this four times.

Date:

Time:

What's the weather like right now?

_____

_____

_____

List three things you can feel:

1
_____

2
_____

3
_____

List five things you can see:

1
_____

2
_____

3
_____

4
_____

5
_____

List two things you can smell:

1
_____

2
_____

List one thing you can taste:

1
_____

List four things you can hear:

1
_____

2
_____

3
_____

4
_____

Breathe in through your nose
for four seconds, and then out
through your mouth
for another four seconds.
Repeat this four times.

Date:

Time:

What's the weather like right now?

_____

_____

_____

List three things you can feel:

1

_____

2

_____

3

_____

List five things you can see:

1

_____

2

_____

3

_____

4

_____

5

_____

List two things you can smell:

1

_____

2

_____

List one thing you can taste:

1

_____

List four things you can hear:

1

_____

2

_____

3

_____

4

_____

Breathe in through your nose
for four seconds, and then out
through your mouth
for another four seconds.
Repeat this four times.